CHAKRA AWAKENING

7 Techniques to Open Your Third Eye Chakra: Guided Meditation for Spiritual Healing and Spiritual Growth

Kate O'Russell

© **Copyright** 2017 by **Kate O'Russell** - All rights reserved.

The following eBook is reproduced below with the goal of providing information that is as accurate and as reliable as possible. Regardless, purchasing this eBook can be seen as consent to the fact that both the publisher and the author of this book are in no way experts on the topics discussed within, and that any recommendations or suggestions made herein are for entertainment purposes only. Professionals should be consulted as needed before undertaking any of the action endorsed herein.

This declaration is deemed fair and valid by both the American Bar Association and the Committee of Publishers Association and is legally binding throughout the United States.

Furthermore, the transmission, duplication or reproduction of any of the following work, including precise information, will be considered an illegal act, irrespective whether it is done electronically or in print. The legality extends to creating a secondary or tertiary copy of the work or a recorded copy and is only allowed with an express written consent of the Publisher. All additional rights are reserved.

The information in the following pages is broadly considered to be a truthful and accurate account of facts, and as such any inattention, use or misuse of the information in question by the reader will render any resulting actions solely under their purview. There are no scenarios in which the publisher or the original author of this work can be in any fashion deemed liable for any hardship or damages that may befall them after undertaking information described herein.

Additionally, the information found on the following pages is intended for informational purposes only and should thus be considered, universal. As befitting its nature, the information presented is without assurance regarding its continued validity or interim quality. Trademarks that mentioned are done without written consent and can in no way be considered an endorsement from the trademark holder.

TABLE OF CONTENTS

INTRODUCTION 1

CHAPTER 1: *What Is Your Third Eye?* 3

CHAPTER 2: *Why Activate Your Third Eye?* 9

CHAPTER 3: *Meditations For The Third Eye* 12

CHAPTER 4 *How To Open Your Third Eye* 25

CHAPTER 5: *Experiences You Might Have* 34

CHAPTER 6: *Healing Your Third Eye* 42

CHAPTER 7: *Increasing Your Clairvoyant Power* 47

CHAPTER 8: *Mistakes To Avoid* 54

CONCLUSION 58

INTRODUCTION

Your "third eye" is considered to be your "spiritual eye" and is a common topic of spiritual awakening. Awakening your third eye enables you to increase your spiritual intuition, your mediumship, and psychic abilities. Individuals who are tuning into their spiritual self for the first time or who are looking to get more in touch with their spiritual self, psychic abilities, and intuition are often encouraged to begin awakening their third eye and learning to activate it easily as an opportunity to increase their skills and abilities.

If you are looking to awaken your third eye, increase your psychic abilities, tap into your intuition, or simply connect further with your spirit, then *Chakra Awakening: 7 Techniques to Open Your Third Eye Chakra: Guided Meditation for Spiritual Healing and Spiritual Growth* is the perfect book for you. This guide will walk you through the process of awakening your third eye and tapping into your natural spiritual abilities with seven different types of meditative exercises and a host of other tips and tricks besides. Each chapter is dedicated to helping you understand your third eye more, connect with it, open it, and learn to activate it effortlessly on command. Being able to be totally connected to and in tune with your third eye means that you will have an increased connection to your spiritual self and your natural and supernatural abilities.

For those who are looking for a complete guide to this process, you have come to the right place. This book will walk you through everything. You will even learn about common symptoms and side effects experienced by those who are going through a spiritual awakening, and what you should expect. By the end of this book, you will have access to all of the information you need in order to activate your third eye, use it, and strengthen it. This book is very comprehensive and will ensure that nothing is left unexplained so that you are capable of having a comfortable and confident awakening.

If you are ready to take the first steps in awakening your third eye, then it is time for you to read on. We will begin with the first chapter where you learn about the third eye in a more in-depth experience and then you will be lead through the remaining chapters that will guide you through the awakening process. Please, take your time and allow yourself to enjoy the experience. This is not one to be rushed.

CHAPTER 1:
What Is Your Third Eye?

The concept of humans having a third eye is rooted in a variety of religions but is most popular in Hinduism. Ultimately, the "third eye" is a mystical "eye" that is rooted slightly above the bridge of your nose, in the center of your forehead. This eye is considered to be an "eye" with metaphysical capabilities.

The third eye is positioned in a place that represents your sixth chakra, or your third eye chakra. It is located directly over the pineal gland, which is believed to be the actual physical basis for what makes the third eye "work". In a non-spiritual text, the third eye is considered the "mind's eye" and is responsible for creating imaginations and mental images. It is believed that the eye can both see outwards and inwards. When it sees outwards, you are experiencing spiritual phenomena. When it sees inward, you are experiencing imagination.

Every person on planet Earth has a third eye, they are not special to any particular individuals or groups of people. However, many people are unaware of its existence, refuse to acknowledge it, or are untrained on how to use it. Those who do learn to tap into this incredible eye are afforded the ability of higher spiritual connection, mediumship abilities, psychic abilities, and other spiritual experiences that are not experienced by those who have not awakened their third eye.

Believe it or not, even those who have yet to awaken their third eye have used it. The third eye speaks through intuition, and virtually everyone has an intuition. If you have ever had a "hunch" or a "feeling" and you followed it and found yourself to be correct in what you expected or believed, then you have listened to and experienced your third eye. This type of experience is a very basic one experienced by the third eye. When you actually take the time to awaken it and tap into its abilities, your hunches become more than just a hunch: they become a sense of all-knowingness, and you learn to intuitively and faithfully follow the "hunches" of your third eye.

Some people call the third eye a "meta organ" because it is a metaphysical part of your body. Even though it is believed to be based on the pineal gland, and it is believed that the pineal gland is responsible for making it work, this has not been confirmed or proven. Instead, many people believe it is a sensory organ that does not actually physically exist, but rather it is a part of your spiritual body.

Your third eye has the power to reveal the all-knowingness of the universe to you. You can learn how to predict future events or circumstances, read other people's energies and vibrations, read energies and vibrations from the spiritual plane, reveal your limiting patterns and behaviors to yourself so you can heal them, and provide you with the knowledge that seems to just "appear" in your mind. There are many different ways that the third eye can benefit you, which is why so many people are inclined to tap into it. This is also why it is commonly discussed in spiritual awakenings, ascension, and other similar topics. Many believe that awakening your third eye is the next logical step in your spiritual journey if you have not already done so. In many cases, they're right. Awakening your third eye can allow you to tap into the full power and potential of your spirit and activate it in a way that cannot be done if you do not take the time to awaken your third eye. In a sense, it is the cord or the connection that exists between your conscious mind and your spiritual self.

As an actual sense, there are many different ways that your third eye can be used. These are called the "clairs" and they are directly related to the third eye. Different people experience different "clairs". Some are stronger in some and weaker in others, some only experience a few, and others experience all of them. Regardless of which you currently experience, you can strengthen your skills with all of them so that you can become better at each one. However, it is always good to know where your strengths and weaknesses lie, as these are where your natural abilities will excel and you will get the best results. The following are the different types of "clairs". There are four major clairs, and 2 minor or less common ones.

Clairvoyance is the most common to be talked about. When you watch TV shows or hear about psychics in popular media whether it's fiction or nonfiction, they are often portrayed to have clairvoyance. These means that they can "see" things as though they are actually happening. The circumstances play out as though they are watching a small movie in their imagination, and then later the circumstances come true in real life. Clairvoyance can be subtle, such as seeing a specific color or aura, or more elaborate such as seeing the entire scene. Some people call these "premonitions", but ultimately what they are talking about is clairvoyance.

Another common one is clairsentience. This skill pertains to those who "feel" things. People who experience clairsentience tend to be empaths, and they can "feel" other people's emotions and feelings as if they are their own. They can also "feel" when something is going to happen. For example, the "hunch" we talked about earlier would be an experience revolving around clairsentience. When it comes to this particular clair, the person experiencing it will not get a vision or anything, they will just get a certain feeling that tells them something will happen. Then, eventually, said thing actually happens.

One ability that is also common is called clairaudience, which means that the individual can hear things. This is not the type of hearing that works within' the physical ears, but rather it is hearing within' the mind. It may sound weird, but to those who experience it, it makes total sense. When you experience clairaudience, it is as though you have heard someone say something, but no one on the physical plane has actually said anything. You might also hear sounds that would not have been related to a person, but still, have no logical root in the physical world. Some people believe these sounds are coming from the spiritual plane and that certain people have the skill of hearing them. If you can hear something with your physical ears, it is not clairaudience. Clairaudience is only the experience that takes place when a sound is heard but there is no logical, physical explanation and it was not heard by the physical ears.

The final common clair is called claircognizance. This is the skill of "clear knowing". When people experience this skill, they seem to know just "know" something, despite never having a firm reason as to why. They do not require logic or facts as a basis for their knowledge, they just know. This is a very common clair, experienced even by many who have yet to awaken their third eye. This is another sense of having a "hunch". For example, let's say something tells you to go a different way to work and you follow that and find later that a major accident happened on your normal route to work. This would be a time where claircognizance was experienced: you "knew" you should do it a different way, and later were proven why your "knowledge" was sound.

Another type of clair that is less common is clairalience. This means that you can smell things that give you certain information. The most common experience with clairalience is when you smell someone who has passed away. You might smell the perfume they wore, or something that reminds you of them or their house. This is a less commonly experienced phenomenon, but many people who do experience it claim it is very relaxing and helps them feel more at peace.

The other less common clair is clairgustance. This means that you can taste things that aren't actually in your mouth. This type of experience is not as common, but it can happen. The most commonly recalled time when this happens is when mediums are communicating with spirit and can literally taste what the spirit's favorite food was. Alternatively, you might think about something and then be able to actually taste it in your mouth. Or, the taste may seem to appear out of nowhere.

All of these experiences are psychic experiences that are recognized and enhanced when people take the time to actually awaken their third eye and strengthen their abilities. You may experience one or more of these already, and when you tap into your third eye you will gain the ability to have greater control over the experiences, even learning to summon them on command. The fact that we all experience at least one of these proves that everyone has a third eye, but only some will choose to actually awaken it and connect to it in order to increase their innate talents. If you are choosing to awaken yours, the rest of this guide will teach you exactly how you can do just that.

CHAPTER 2:
Why Activate Your Third Eye?

Many people are unclear as to what the true benefits of awakening your third eye are. If you can already use it despite not having to actually try, then what is the point? Aren't you already "awakened"? The answer to this is somewhat complex, but also fairly straightforward. We are going to go ahead and explore it, now.

To answer the first part of the question: just because you are using your third eye does not mean you have mastered it. Your third eye should be seen as a muscle of sorts: the more you exercise it, the stronger it gets. While you can continue to use it as you always have, consciously taking control and using it intentionally can help you increase the strength in your third eye and therefore have greater success when using it. You develop a greater sense of confidence in the information you receive when working with your activated third eye, and you are able to lead a life that is more aligned with what feels right for you.

Another reason why people should awaken their third eye completely is so that they are not persuaded by the truths of others. Although it is believed that the universal truth remains the same for all, each individual has their own truth, as well. If you do not take the time to activate your third eye, then you will never know exactly what your individual truth is. As a result, you may never get to live up to your full potential, tap into your full capabilities, or share your purpose with the world. You may, instead, end up living a mediocre life following the rules set forth by someone else. We end up becoming "sheep" in a sense.

One speculation suggests that because we are all slowly becoming more aware of our spiritual selves and spiritual abilities, then we are all becoming awakened. However, it is important to understand that there are varying levels of "awakened". Those who are recently paying attention to their awakened state and waking up to the truth, for example, will not know quite as much as those who have been at it for a while. It takes time for people to fully awaken and shed the limiting beliefs and structures that have been forced on them by society. Once they do, however, they can live in total alignment with their respective truth.

When you are becoming awakened, you may notice that you are more and more awakened with each passing day. The more you learn about yourself, humanity, the universe and spirit, the more awakened you become. You learn more about the universal truth, your own truth, and what life is truly all about. We stop living lives that are commanded by others, and we start commanding our own lives. Life becomes more freeing, more purposeful, and fuller of intention. We lead lives that are more satisfying, more fulfilling, and more aligned with what we truly came here to do. We stop worrying about what others think or what we think we are supposed to do and we start doing what we know to be right, based on our own personal truths.

Awakening your third eye is not only about tapping into your natural psychic abilities, but it is also about allowing yourself the freedom to live the life you came here to live. You learn more about yourself than you ever would without awakening your third eye, and you step further into your power and your ability to do what you came to this Earth to do. You are no longer held down by the fear, hate, anger, despair and other miserable emotions that tend to be free-floating around the Earth, and instead, you tune into peace, love, and happier vibrations that serve you on a higher level. As a result, you can serve the universe on a higher level, and the entire Earth ascends just a little more. The more we all ascend, such as through awakening our third eyes, the more elevated Earth becomes and the more peaceful and loving our planet becomes.

Awakening your third eye, then, is not just about you. It is about what you can offer for yourself, and what you can offer for all of the humanity. It goes much beyond who you are as an individual and allows you to contribute to humanity on a global level. When you combine the two factors: the fact that you will lead a happier, more purposeful and enjoyable life, and the fact that you will be contributing to global elevation, you can see that awakening your third eye is an incredibly important spiritual process that everyone should undergo when they are ready. It is an extremely incredible experience, and you will likely find that life becomes much more enjoyable and meaningful after you have undergone the process of awakening your third eye. Once the door is open, it's almost impossible to close it off again.

CHAPTER 3:
Meditations For The Third Eye

One of the best ways to begin the awakening process for your third eye is to meditate. If you have already practiced meditating in the past, then you may have experienced energy or vibrations in the third eye area. If not, then this may be new to you. Either way, we are going to explore how meditating can help you awaken the third eye.

Before You Begin

Before you begin the process of meditating, you should know that this process is going to be very personal. While there are general guides you can follow to help you focus on the third eye and the actual awakening process, everyone's unique experiences and visions will be different from one another. You may have similar experiences to other people, but you likely won't have the exact same thing. This is because each person is unique and has their own natural talents and strengths when it comes to psychic topics. Remember the clairs we talked about in the last chapter? You will likely notice your unique clair strengths activating during your meditation process. You may also feel the awakening of other strengths that you didn't necessarily know you had or that you haven't experienced before. The entire process can be very exciting, but it can also be intense if you have never experienced anything like it before.

Getting Ready

Prior to the process of beginning your meditations, make sure that you prepare yourself for the meditation process. You can do this by finding a comfortable place to sit or lie down where you aren't going to be interrupted. This process could take anywhere from fifteen minutes to an hour, or maybe even longer. Ideally, you should have at least an hour of alone, uninterrupted time so that you don't feel like you have to rush the process. Make sure your phone and any other distractions are turned off or are removed from the vicinity so you can stay very focused on your meditation and don't become distracted by anything in the room.

In addition to eliminating distractions and setting aside time for your meditation, you want to prepare yourself physically. Ultimately, you want to do whatever it is that will make you extremely calm and relaxed in the moment. Wear clothes that are loose fitting and that won't cause you to feel itchy, constricted, or otherwise uncomfortable. Make sure you have a light blanket handy, as you don't want to catch a chill. Avoid having too heavy of a blanket, however, because you also don't want to become too hot. You might consider having some relaxing music on in the background, such as binaural beats specific to relaxation or third eye awakening, or other soft background music. Make sure the music is free of words. Sometimes having this can help you ignore background noise that may be going on around you, such as people outside your window or neighbors in your apartment building. If you would like to light some candles or warm some incense, you can do this also. Consider using aromas specific to the third eye, such as rosemary, patchouli, or frankincense. Make sure you check the guidelines on the aromas so you don't use ones that may be harmful to you if you or someone in your home has particular health concerns.

Getting yourself really comfortable and relaxed is a great way to ensure that you will be able to fully focused inward during your meditation experience. The calmer you are, the more focused you will be because you will not be concerned about any discomforts you are experiencing physically during your meditation. If you were to prefer, you could even do this meditation in a quiet meadow, park, or elsewhere. Make sure if you are doing it outdoors that you are safe from wildlife or any other potential dangers, as you will want to be focused inward and not subjecting yourself to the potential harms of your environment.

Before you actually begin the meditation process, even before the first few deep breaths, take some time to sit down in your relaxing environment and take it all in. If you sit there for a few minutes after preparing it, it will help you to further relax so that your experience is that much more effective and enjoyable. Furthermore, it will help you identify if anything is not quite to your liking, so you can adjust everything before you begin. If you are using a blanket, make sure you have that over you during the preparation process. After a few minutes of relaxing, you should know whether it is going to be too hot or too cold for your meditation.

Meditation Style One - Gentle Awakening (10-15 minutes)

The first meditation is very fluid. This is for people who don't typically like to be guided or pushed through a process but would rather experience it naturally as it happens. For this meditation, you want to start by getting comfortable and then taking a few deep breaths. Always breathe through your nose. If you would like, you can exhale through your mouth, though this is not necessary. Do what is most comfortable for you.

Once you have taken a few deep breaths, close your eyes. Count out five more deep breaths, and feel yourself falling deeper into a state of relaxation with each exhale, and into a higher state of being with each inhale.

When you have finished your five breaths, set the intention that you want to explore your third eye, and that you desire to awaken it. Then, let go of this intention and any expectations of how the experience is going to go. Over the next several moments you will likely be focusing more on your third eye, so you will notice any sensations or experiences that take place in this area. Pay attention to your thoughts and visions, also. If you notice your thoughts are going too far away from your intention, gently draw them back towards your peace, and then let your mind wander again as it heads back towards your third eye.

This meditation is great for those who are just beginning to explore their third eye or those who have already been exploring it but want to further explore it. You may experience an awakening during this process, but generally, it is more about exploring the area. This in and of itself is a part of the awakening process, so it is extremely beneficial for virtually anyone, regardless of how much or little experience you have working with your third eye. If you set the intention right and explore this meditation on a regular basis, you can awaken your third eye completely over time. Continue this process until your mind starts to wander, once this occurs it is better to end your meditation as opposed to attempting to force the results you are looking for. Try to build your meditation tolerance so that you are able to last between 10 and 15 minutes before moving on to more advanced meditation styles.

Meditation Style Two - Guided Awakening (10-15 minutes)

This awakening is for those who are looking for a little more guidance and focal points during their meditation. Sometimes just letting your mind wander can take you anywhere but where you want to go. If this feels like the truth for you, then you might want to consider using the following meditation style. Begin by relaxing in your comfortable place and taking several deep breaths in through your nose.

Once you have reached a relaxed state, gently close your eyes and take five more deep breaths. Each time you breathe in, imagine you are ascending to your higher self and each time you breathe out, imagine you are becoming twice as more relaxed.

After you have completed your five breaths, focus on your third eye area. Notice any sensations you are feeling in the area. If you are having any visions in your mind, notice them. For a few minutes, take the time to just explore this area.

Once you have familiarized yourself with the sensations associated with your third eye, imagine you can see a large closed eye over this area. When you are ready, imagine the eye opening up. As it opens, envision a bright light beaming from the eye, turning the world before you to a beautiful indigo hue. Indigo is the color of the third eye chakra. Allow the eye to continue opening and beaming this bright indigo light until it is extremely bright and powerful. The light should not flicker, should not be faded, and should appear to be beaming to its fullest. Allow the light to beam for a while. As you do, take the time to explore any new sensations, feelings, or visions that may arise. Sit with them until you have familiarized yourself with these new experiences.

When you are ready, thank your third eye, and then take five deep breaths. Each time, imagine your physical body awakening from the meditation a little more, and you return back to your physical body.

After your breaths, gently shake off your body and complete your meditation process. Continue this process until your mind starts to wander, once this occurs it is better to end your meditation as opposed to attempting to force the results you are looking for. Try to build your meditation tolerance so that you are able to last between 10 and 15 minutes before moving on to more advanced meditation styles.

This meditation is great for those who are awakening their third eye for the first time. When you have already awakened your third eye, you may find that sometimes it isn't as open as it has been in the past. This can happen when we don't pay much attention to the third eye, and we let it "slip", per se. Using this meditation is a great way to allow your third eye to regain full strength so that you can continue using it to the maximum of its abilities.

These two meditation styles are great for those who are looking to awaken their third eye chakra. When you use them, you can feel your third eye opening and begin to explore what it feels like when your third eye has been awakened. You might notice that your sensations alter from time to time, and this is normal. Like humans, the strengths and skills associated with your third eye can evolve and grow. You will notice these from time to time and should take the time to explore them so you can stay fully connected to your third eye.

When you have awakened your third eye, you can also meditate to maintain its awakened state. Basic meditations where you simply close your eyes and focus on the present moment can be great for this process. You can also use the aforementioned meditations as an opportunity to increase its strength and ensure it stays open to its fullest state. When you are connected to your third eye and really tune in, it will tell you what it needs in order for you to stay fully connected.

Meditation is the best way to awaken your third eye and should be the first part of the process when you are getting started. If you dislike meditation, take it slow and do a little more each time. This will ensure that you are staying focused and that you are not becoming stressed. If the process becomes stressful or uncomfortable to you in any way, then you are not going to get the most out of it and you will struggle to succeed with the awakening process through meditation. Be sure to take your time and do it at the pace of your own unique journey. A large part of being awakened is honoring that no two journeys are the same, and what works for you may work differently or not at all for others. Honor that in yourself and in humanity.

Meditation Style Three – Seeing Through Your Third Eye Meditation

This can be an extremely powerful type of meditation, especially when practiced in the presence of a master, or if you have previously worked with a master or watched their videos, a picture of their face. You are going to want to start by mentally and physically preparing yourself as you would for any meditative exercise and by clearing your mind of aberrant thoughts. Once you are ready to begin, the first phase of this type of meditation should last for about five minutes.

You will want to close your eyes and look for the first picture that appears in your mind's eye. Really focus on this image and give it your full attention. Work on bringing it into as stark of relief as possible, focus on even the smallest details until you can see them in absolute clarity. It should ideally feel as though you should be able to reach out and touch whatever it is that you are visualizing.

Once you have focused on your mental picture for five minutes, the next step should also last for about five minutes.

You will now want to open your eyes along with your third eye and stare directly into either your master's eyes or the eyes of the master in the picture. Don't just look at the eyes, look through them, feel the power they contain and think of all the wisdom and energy that they contain. Focus on the feeling that the master's words have had on you and do everything in your power to either connect with them on another level or to visualize them as if they were in the room with you. Repeat this process a second time before repeating the first step a third time.

After this you should feel a strong tingling sensation in the middle of your forehead, this is your third eye feeling fully energized and ready to help you in whatever ways you need most.

Meditation Style Four – Physical Object Focus Meditation (10 minutes)

When you are first beginning your journey towards awakening your third eye through meditation, you will likely regularly feel your mind begin to wander. In order to counter this tendency, you may find it helpful to add a physical focal point to your meditation in order to keep your mind as focused on the present as possible. Candles are a common meditation tool as the flickering flame provides enough movement to hold the eye without being distracting enough to make the entire meditative process more difficult. You are going to want to start by mentally and physically preparing yourself as you would for any meditative exercise and by clearing your mind of aberrant thoughts.

With your object in the room, you are going to want to choose a mantra that speaks to you for this specific meditative session. You can say your mantra mentally or aloud, what really matters is that it is something personal that really speaks to you. The phrase you speak should be something that you are currently working to integrate into your mind or a way in which you are striving to improve your awareness.

If you are saying it aloud, you will want to say it once while you inhale, and again when you exhale, taking care that it doesn't stop you from taking deep, measured breaths.

With a mantra in mind, you are then going to want to repeat it to yourself constantly until you feel as though you can internalize the message. As you do so, you will want to alternate between staring at the candle with your eyes open for two minutes and then closing your eyes and trying to visualize the candle for another two minutes. Repeat this cycle five times, keeping your mantra up the entire time.

During the process, you should begin to feel a tingling in the middle of your forehead. When you do, try and connect it to the thought of the flame, fanning both with your energy.

Meditation Method Five – Gathering Energy (20 minutes)

This type of meditation is great for supercharging your third eye before you know you are going to really need to put it to good use. You are going to want to stretch before you begin this meditative exercise in order to ensure that you are in the proper state for meditation. You will want to bend over and touch your toes, raise your arms high above your head, and then lay on your back with your legs straight out above you, each for about 30 seconds. With this done, you are going to want to start by mentally and physically preparing yourself as you would for any meditative exercise and by clearing your mind of aberrant thoughts.

To start this meditative exercise, you will want to sit cross-legged on the floor in a relaxed position. Don't get too relaxed, however, as you will need to ensure that your back is straight and your chest is open and your head upright and fully supported. Once you are in the proper position you are going to want to breathe deeply in a regular pattern and concentrate on relaxing as much as possible.

Once you have reached a state of true relaxation, the next thing you are going to want to do is to count backward slowly, starting with the number one hundred, you are going to want to picture each number briefly for about five seconds in your mind before moving on to the next. While at first, you will likely feel nothing, as you continue the exercise you should feel your third eye begin to open and then grow more and more charged with energy. As this occurs you will want to connect the energy to the visualization, urging it to grow brighter and brighter with each number.

You will know you have completed the exercise when you can feel it practically coursing with untapped energy.

Meditation Method Six – Sight Unseen Meditation (10 minutes)

This is a great type of practical meditation that will help to naturally improve your perception at all times, regardless of when you last practiced meditation. This is because it will help you to start avoiding many of the filters that most people naturally put up in order to go about their day to day lives in an uninterrupted fashion. You are going to want to start by mentally and physically preparing yourself as you would for any meditative exercise and by clearing your mind of aberrant thoughts.

To begin, you will want to find a relaxed position with your right arm stretched out in such a way that it parallels the floor and your elbow is extended fully. You will want to ensure your right palm is facing up and your fingers are in a cupped position. With your left hand, you will want to ensure your thumb and the third finger are lightly touching while the arm is positioned so the elbow is at your side and your forearm is facing out.

Once in the proper position, you will want to focus all of your concentration on the very point of your chin while repeating the mantra Wahe Guru" (Wha-hey-goo-roo). Repeat for ten minutes before flexing both of your hands and inhaling while turning to the left and then repeating the process while turning to the right.

CHAPTER 4
How To Open Your Third Eye

Opening your third eye takes time and practice. While you may have an experience, such as during meditation, where you feel a huge rush of awakening, it will not be fully awakened by one experience. Rather, the awakening is a process and you must take your time and commit to it if you are going to experience a full awakening.

Beginning with meditation is a great way to start opening your third eye, but there are additional ways that you can open it as well. In this chapter, we are going to explore the other ways that you can open your third eye, in addition to meditation. Some of these are practices that you must set aside time for, while others are ones that you can use in your regular daily life. As you are using these practices, it is important to understand that your third eye awakening will be a very spiritual and individual process, but having it in an awakened state means that you are going to integrate it into your daily life. Awakening your third eye should not consume all of your time and result in you doing nothing but focusing on the awakened state of your third eye. Rather, you should set aside some time but otherwise focus on leading your life as you normally would. As your third eye awakens, you will notice differences about yourself that stem from this awakening process.

However, you should continue leading your daily life and allowing these changes to naturally integrate, rather than forcing them. Anything forced is not natural, and therefore may inhibit the opening process for your third eye.

Learn to Silence Your Mind

In addition to proper meditation, practice silencing your mind. When we go about our daily lives, there tends to be a lot of chatter and noise in our minds that can keep us constantly distracted and focused on everything except what we are doing. A great way to support your third eye awakening is to learn to silence your mind and focus only on the task at hand. When you do, your mind will be focused, and the background will be silenced. It is typically within' these silences that the third eye and our psychic abilities will kick in and take place.

While it is impossible to entirely stop thinking, you should stay very intentional with your thinking process and focus specifically on what you need to be thinking about depending on what you are physically doing. The third eye chakra tends to "activate" and work during the "in between" times that take place between thoughts and experiences. Therefore, if you want to intentionally activate it, you need to intentionally set aside space for these in-between moments to happen. When you do, make sure that you are paying attention and are aware of when they happen so that you can focus on them and practice strengthening your ability to activate them whenever you desire.

Practice Tuning In

If modern society has taught us anything, it's that we should ignore the little voice inside and do what's "right" based on what others have told us to believe is right. We are often lead astray from our intuition, and therefore we struggle to actually listen to it. If you will recall, your intuition is your third eye speaking to you. If you want to awaken your third eye and help it open further, you need to focus on eliminating the desire to ignore this voice and actually tune into it.

When you feel or hear something coming from your intuition, take the time to acknowledge it, and then actually listen to it. Do whatever it says, and then notice what happens as a result. In many instances life becomes easier, a hazard is avoided, we recognize or learn something we may have missed, or things are otherwise "better" overall. Sometimes these realizations may not be as obvious, but they do exist. Learning to tune into your intuition means you are learning to acknowledge and give credit to your third eye. And, as the saying says "where your attention goes, energy flows" which means that if you are intentionally listening to your third eye and your intuition, it will continue speaking to you. The more you tune in and listen, the better your "relationship" or connection will be, and the better results you will get from tuning in.

Explore Your Natural Creativity

Our creative sides are largely linked to our third eye. Those who are highly creative tend to be very creative, or interested in increasing their creative abilities. If you want to connect closer to your third eye, practice embracing your creativity and letting it free. Even if you don't think you are a good artist or you are inexperienced with various art forms, practice them anyway. Let your imagination take over and create anything that comes to mind. Don't hold expectations of what it should or shouldn't look like, just create. You will find that when you do this, your third eye chakra will feel more enhanced naturally. Remember, your third eye is also your "mind's eye" which means that it is your imagination. When you create from your imagination, you are directly creating from your third eye. It can be an incredible experience alongside your awakening process.

Take Time to Ground Yourself

Your third eye can take you into the spiritual realm through your mind's eye and your intuition, and when you are not careful it can affect your ability to stay grounded. When you are working with your third eye, you should be simultaneously working with your root chakra and grounding yourself. You can do this by meditating on your root chakra and imagine actual etheric roots connecting you to the center of the Earth. This is a great way to counterbalance your third eye and keep you rooted while also allowing you to explore your awakening.

When you don't take the time to root yourself, you can experience what is known as "overstimulation", which means your third eye is working more than your other chakras. This can lead to stress, discomfort, being overwhelmed, and many other unwanted experiences. When the process of awakening becomes uncomfortable, people are more likely to avoid it and therefore they can find themselves not wanting to further their awakening. Furthermore, they might shut their eye out of fear and have difficulty wanting to return to the awakening process at any point in the future. To avoid being overwhelmed and the discomfort, make sure you are always focusing on grounding yourself. If you are not a major fan of meditation, you can also allow your bare feet to connect directly to the Earth, as this is a great physical grounding process.

Exercise Your Third Eye

Exercising your third eye is a great way to help support its opening. It also increases your strength and abilities, meaning you will have an easier time keeping it open, using it on a regular basis, and activating your psychic abilities at any time which you desire. The following are great exercises you can practice to help you support your third eye opening.

One great way is to do meditations that involve all of the chakras. Similar to how it is important to ground and focus on your root chakra, you should also focus on strengthening your other chakras, too. While you may wish to primarily focus on strengthening and growing your abilities with them one at a time, it is important that you continue to give focus to each of them. As previously stated, when one or two chakras become overstimulated from being used more than the others, it can create a spiritual imbalance that can create unwanted side effects for the individual. A great meditation is to lay down and meditate, then imagine your chakras one at a time. Start with your root chakra and work your way up to your crown chakra. As you go, imagine each one shining brighter and brighter until it is shining its brightest. You can also imagine them spinning clockwise, as they are a fluid energy that moves, they do not simply beam like a lamp, but rather swirl like a whirlpool.

Another great way to work with your third eye is to do dream work. Using lucid dreaming meditations, and practicing dream interpretation are both great ways to practice dream work. Lucid dreaming is typically completed using meditations, where you allow yourself to go into a dream state and then you mentally control yourself in the dream state. It allows you to be in control of your dream, rather than your dream be in control like they typically are. Dream interpretation itself requires you to allow the dream to flow naturally, and then you interpret it upon waking up. The best way to do this is to write about your dream in the moments after you have woken up. You can then interpret them on your own, or purchase a dream interpretation journal to help you interpret different elements within' the dream.

Allowing your imagination to flow naturally and on its own is another great way to play with your third eye. Practice sitting in a meditative state, and then let your imagination flow. Just follow it anywhere it goes. During this type of meditation, there is no need to draw your attention back to any particular place, you can simply let it go to wherever it desires to be. You can also allow your imagination to flow while you are creating such as through drawing, writing, pottery, or other crafts. Allowing your meditation to take charge and faithfully following it can help you feel more connected to your third eye, and can help support its awakening.

Intuition lead breaks are another great way to strengthen your third eye. Like with playing with your imagination, you are letting your intuition lead the way. This means that you go anywhere and do anything that your intuition is telling you to. So, if your intuition tells you to go sit by a particular tree in a certain park and look in a certain direction, you do it. When you follow your intuition this way, you leave yourself open to receiving mental "downloads" that are often filled with information that can be beneficial to your present state. You might learn something about yourself, be guided to take a specific action in a certain situation, or otherwise feel lead to do something. All of these stem from your third eye guidance and should be honored when you experience them during this time. If you will recall, honoring your intuition is a great way to activate and increase the strength of your third eye.

The final best way to exercise your third eye is to strengthen your psychic abilities. Whenever you experience one of the clairs, allow yourself to fully embrace it. If it is showing you something or encouraging you to do something or trust a certain piece of information with no logical explanation, do your best to follow it. When you do, you will be strengthening the ability and your connection to your third eye.

Opening your third eye is a process. There is the process of opening it for the first time, and then the process of keeping it open. When you nurture your third eye, you will find that life is incredible and much simpler than you may have ever believed it could be. Our third eye can be considered our own built-in "northern star" guiding us in the direction we need to go. When we follow it and we listen to what it has to say, we are naturally guided to where we need to be in order to have the best experiences.

You have likely had many instances where you followed your third eye's guidance without knowing it since your third eye speaks to you through your intuition. When you open it intentionally, however, it becomes easier to follow and explore intentionally, and not go in a different direction because of any fear you may have of listening to your inner voice. When you are not intentionally listening to it and are unaware of the power of your third eye, it can be easy to be led astray and then end up feeling guilty or out of place because you did something you did not want to or that was not good for you despite something inside you telling you that you should have never done it in the first place.

When you are opening your third eye, ensure that you set aside time to continue doing it. There may be times where you don't always focus on it, but overall you should invest a few hours per week on working with your third eye chakra. This will help ensure that you are staying connected with it and that it is serving you in the most powerful way possible. As a result, you will find that life is much more balanced, fulfilling, satisfying, and purposeful. You will find more meaning in your life, and you will find that it is easier to follow your internal compass without fear that you are doing the wrong thing. In fact, you will have a much easier time being yourself, and the judgment and beliefs of others will not have such a strong ability to impact your own beliefs and you will be able to feel much freer.

CHAPTER 5:
Experiences You Might Have

When you open your third eye, many things can happen. You will have wonderful experiences, and you may have some "side effects" as well. Although your experience is going to be unique to you, there are some commonly talked about events that occur when people open their third eye. Here's what you can expect.

How You Feel Within' Will Change

When you awaken your third eye, the way you feel inside will change. If you have been feeling out of alignment, as though you are living someone else's reality, or otherwise disconnected from yourself and your purpose, this will all change. When you start to listen to your intuition and follow it, you allow yourself to have a greater connection with yourself. Everything inside that you ever wanted and felt like doing will start to be honored, and the connection you experience with yourself will change your inner world. Any feelings of guilt, disconnect, fear, or loss that you may have felt as a result of not living in alignment with your true self will fade as you begin to connect to your own inner world and honor yourself. Most people report feeling as though they are living a more authentic and enjoyable life because they are no longer concerned about other people and judgments. Instead, they are only concerned with their own judgment of themselves, and about living a life that genuinely feels good for them.

You Might Lose Touch with Reality

Some people experience overstimulation with their third eye, and they may slightly lose touch with reality. You will need to practice grounding and connecting to your root chakra to avoid this experience. When you lose touch with your reality, it might feel like you are slipping a little. You may struggle to have connections with people in the real world or to maintain relationships with others. If you are spending too much time working with your third eye and paying attention to your psychic abilities, you may feel an entire disconnect from reality and feel as though you are living out of alignment all over again, only in an entirely new way. If you feel this is happening, you can stop it or prevent it by connecting with your root chakra and grounding yourself. You may want to refrain from working with your third eye for a day or two while you reconnect with your physical reality and learn to create a healthy balance between the two realities you now live within'.

You Will Have Psychic Experiences

The entire point of opening your third eye is typically to increase your psychic abilities and learn how to work with them on the physical plane. As a result, you are going to start experiencing psychic abilities. A reason why this is on this list, however, is because some people are not prepared for what life is like when your psychic abilities are activated. At first, before you learn to control your psychic abilities and live with a balance between your third eye and your root chakras, you may experience "out of control" moments with your psychic abilities. You may have an overwhelming number of visions, your intuition may seem to speak *a lot,* and you might otherwise feel overwhelmed by the number of your psychic episodes.

This can happen in the beginning, and it can happen if your third eye ever becomes overstimulated. The best thing you can do is refrain from intentionally working with your third eye for a few days, and focus on intentionally quieting your mind. Set the intention that you will not have any psychic experiences unless you are welcoming them or they are necessary, and then let your mind come to a resting silence. Just like we must learn to silence our conscious mind from chatter relating to our physical existence, we also have to learn to silence our subconscious mind from chatter relating to our psychic abilities. Practice balance and you will notice these symptoms subside and you regain control.

You Will Feel Aligned with The Universe

Feeling aligned with the universe is potentially one of the greatest parts of opening up your third eye. You feel as though you have an innate understanding of things you don't even know about, and that everything is in perfect alignment. You might start noticing universal messages through numerology or other symbols that you learn about as you explore the spiritual plane. You may also feel as though no coincidences are happening but rather everything is perfectly playing out in your favor. Sometimes you might feel as though things are against you and it may test your faith in the universe. If you remain faithful, it will soon make sense as to why you are having all of the experiences you are experiencing.

Feeling aligned with the universe can help you understand that there is something greater than you in the world and that you are fully supported and loved by that greater something. This feeling is unexplainable and can only be experienced when you open your third eye. The connection and synchronicity you feel are incredible, intense, and very powerful. You will never have an experience like it without the connection to the universe.

You Might See Things That Aren't Technically There

One common thing that people say when they activate their third eye is seeing things that aren't technically there. This is different than clairvoyance because you are not having mental visions, but rather you are seeing something with your physical eyes. The most common ones that people claim to see include streaks or spots of white sparkling light, auras, energy frequencies or microscopic colorful sparkles in the air, streaks of blue or purple light, and other similar things. These are not typically seen by those who have not awakened their third eye, but they become extremely common once you have. There is no real explanation for these experiences, but many people claim that they believe it because they are now physically seeing the spiritual plane that lives amongst our physical reality. Those who are awakened can sometimes see these spiritual phenomena with their physical eyes, which is a truly exceptional experience.

Your Meditation Could Deepen and Change

When you awaken your third eye, there is a good chance that how you experience meditation will change. It may suddenly become easier to meditate in a deeper state for a longer time, or you may find that you have more vivid visions in your mind. You may even feel called to meditate more frequently, or at specific times. These "callings" may happen out of the blue and prompt you to meditate immediately, or they may simply urge you to meditate soon. They may even simply be calling you to meditate more frequently than you already are, or focus on something in particular when you meditate. Meditation when you have awakened your third eye changes. You go from meditating just to clear your mind, to meditating to both clear your mind *and* connect with your spiritual self and the universe. The quality of your meditation will change as a result, and so will the experiences you have while meditating.

Unexplained Euphoria

Many people report feeling unexplained feelings of euphoria when they have awakened their third eye. There are many reasons as to why this may happen, but we cannot be completely sure, of course. Some speculate that when you connect to the universe and your higher self, you feel extreme relief from the unrealistic standards and expectations of society and this relief can lead to a sense of euphoria. Others claim that when you have been "lost" for so long, finding your way back to your true self can lead to a great sense of euphoria when you feel the connection. Regardless, there is a good chance that you may feel an unexplained state of euphoria following the awakening of your third eye.

Heightened Emotions

Many people experience heightened emotions when they have awakened their third eye. For example, when someone else is having a hard time, you might feel as though you want to cry for them when previously you didn't cry much. Alternatively, you may feel the urge to cry, laugh, or otherwise express emotions in a very strong way that you have never experienced before. If you are not prepared for this or are not aware of this symptom, it may feel as though you have lost your wits and you are having an emotional breakdown. The reality is that this is simply you awakening to your true self and fully unleashing all elements of yourself. When you awaken your third eye, every part of yourself awakens. This includes your spiritual body *and* your emotional body where you may have been numbing out things for a long period of time. When you awaken yourself, the numbness wears off and you begin to feel the emotions you have repressed for a long time.

If you are struggling with negative emotions, in particular, you might consider doing intentional healing work. We will discuss more on this in the next chapter, but ultimately it focuses on you healing your soul and emotions in a very intentional way that helps prevent you from feeling as though you are spiraling out of control.

Physical Symptoms

Something that surprises many people is that you can also experience physical symptoms when you awaken your third eye. Many people are unaware of this possibility because the third eye is connected to the soul, but you should understand that the third eye is actually the mind-body connector. As a result, you can certainly have very physical symptoms to your third eye awakening. Some of these symptoms include things like headaches, pressure around the third eye area, cramps, and fatigue. Others may be more uncomfortable like diarrhea, upset stomach, lowered digestive abilities, lowered immune system, and a slower metabolism. Once you have fully embraced the transition and you have reached a state of mind-body balance through the third eye chakra and grounding, these symptoms should subside. In the meantime, take it easy on yourself and do what you can to nurture your body through this process so that you can experience some relief from these symptoms.

In addition to these symptoms, you may experience many others as a result of your third eye opening. If you are experiencing any that haven't been explained, write them down in a journal. Do this for several days, and then look back at the trends. This is a great way to see what is going on and what might be triggering the symptoms, but it can also give you a wonderful opportunity to work with your third eye intentionally. You can look back at these symptoms and take the time to activate your third eye and "ask" yourself what might be causing these symptoms and how you can manage them. Then, through your intuition, your third eye will "answer". It may take some time and you might have to meditate on the question, but the answer should arise. This is a great way to start practicing building your connection with your third eye and intentionally tapping into your intuition.

CHAPTER 6:
Healing Your Third Eye

Once you have awakened your third eye, you have awakened all aspects of yourself. This means that things you may have repressed, such as memories or emotions, may come back and you might experience them with a particularly heightened sense of emotions. This can be really exhausting and difficult, and if you aren't intentionally focusing on healing, it can be overwhelming. You might find that you feel as though you are drowning in your emotions and pain because you feel as though you have no control over it. Things that you have not thought about in a long time may arise, causing you to wonder where they have come from, and the entire experience can be very difficult.

When you awaken your third eye, you should be prepared to heal yourself from these things. How much you experience will depend on your unique life circumstances, but virtually everyone has some level of healing to do. Since we are discussing how you can awaken your third eye, we also want to discuss how you can heal it. This will ensure that the process is enjoyable and has a positive outcome and that you are not overwhelmed, distraught, or regretful over your choice of opening your third eye.

Journal

Journaling is one of the best ways to start the healing process. This allows you to further explore the feelings you are experiencing, and to document them as well. When you journal, it helps get things off of your chest and out into the open - in a controlled manner. It also gives you the opportunity to really explore what the root of the emotions are, and why they are hurting you so terribly. You might want to purchase a journal specifically for this because you will likely be surprised by the amount of stuff that comes up. Often times people draw experiences from their childhood and other areas of their lives that they thought they had dealt with when they, in fact, hadn't. This is an opportunity to officially let everything out, see it for what it is, and work through it. You will likely be drawn through many lessons when you journal. Once you get these things out of your mind and have explored them, you give yourself the chance to see the *true* "issue" and heal it appropriately.

Focus on One at A Time

It can be very hard to try and heal all of your emotions and pains at once, so it is best that you heal everything one at a time. Imagine as though your emotions are swords. If you try and pick all of them up at once you are going to get stabbed and hurt by them. If you pick one up at a time and carefully take care of it before going to the next, however, you will be less likely to get severely injured and it will be much easier to manage. Try and focus one at a time. Look at the one that is troubling you the most, and focus on that one. You will likely find that the emotions you *think* are the most troubling stem from other emotions, so it may take a little digging to find out what the *true* root problem emotion is. Once you have, however, you will be able to heal it and work through the rest of them until you are healed once again. This process can take a long time, so it is important that you take your time and don't rush it. Allow it to take place naturally, and set the intention that you are going to do it in the way that feels best for yourself.

Allow Yourself to Feel

We have been conditioned to bottle up our emotions and as a result, it can be natural to try and deny tears, laughter, anger, or other feelings. If you have a feeling that you want to express, it is important that you let yourself express it. Take time to allow the emotion to flow out naturally. You might have to wait until a better time if you are in a completely inappropriate place to feel certain emotions. For example, you don't want to start crying in the middle of an important business meeting because that might have a negative effect on your career. However, you do want to make sure that you intentionally set aside time to go back, explore that emotion, and allow it to flow out naturally later.

Even after you have healed yourself, you will likely find that you have these urges later on in life. This is because we are regularly being exposed to different emotional triggers, new hurts, and other such things. Learning to effectively feel your emotions without bottling them up is the best way to ensure that you are continuously healing and that you aren't restricting yourself from the healing process. If you do, you might inadvertently close your third eye once again.

Ask Your Third Eye for Help

Many people aren't aware of the fact that you can ask your third eye for help when you are healing from the pain that arises with your third eye awakening. As you are healing, ask it to guide you and give you signs as to what you can do to increase your healing. You can also ask where certain emotions are coming from, for guidance to getting to the root of the problem, and for assistance in focusing on one at a time. There are many ways that you can ask your third eye for help. Believe it or not, your third eye *wants* you to heal from these emotions. It may not feel like it when you are being overwhelmed by them, but this feeling of overwhelm is typically the result of you not listening to your intuition or your third eye. When you do, it will guide you through the entire process in a way that is relieving and satisfying, instead of painful and overwhelming. While you will still feel the pain, you will be able to feel it actually releasing, rather than simply feel as though you are getting lost in it. Let your third eye and intuition help you through the process and it will become much easier.

Consider A Mentor

You might consider talking to someone who has also experienced their third eye opening. Since virtually everyone has some level of healing to do, talking to someone who has already been through it can be very helpful. People who have truly opened their third eye tend to be very compassionate and are willing to listen and offer support and advice through this process. Sometimes, just being heard by someone who understands can have a very therapeutic effect when it comes to the healing process.

Healing your third eye isn't always fun, but it is a very necessary part of awakening your third eye. Once you awaken it, you will "see" every part of yourself, even the stuff you tried to hide for fear of the pain or other difficult emotions that are associated with it. When you awaken yourself, these are going to come to the surface. It is important that you are prepared to work towards healing them so that you can feel the true euphoria and joy that can be experienced when you are awakened and fully connected to your higher self and the universe.

CHAPTER 7:
Increasing Your Clairvoyant Power

You likely want to awaken your third eye as an opportunity to increase your psychic abilities. The most intriguing one that virtually everyone wants to tap into and experience seems to be clairvoyance, or the skill of being able to clearly see things before they happen, within' the mind's eye. This is an incredible skill that can be very helpful and can increase your feeling of connection with your higher self and the universe.

With clairvoyance, you really want to pay attention to strengthening your imagination muscle. This is the part where your clairvoyant "messages" will come through. The more you work together with your imagination, the more you are going to be able to use it and therefore the easier it will be to receive your visual messages. The following activities are a great way to help enhance your imagination and open yourself up to receiving clairvoyant messages.

Once you have strengthened this muscle, you will likely find that you can "see" things on a regular basis. For example, you might look at an old house or photograph and be able to "see" what took place there or what was happening there at a time in the past. You may be able to hold an old locket and "see" the person who once wore it or "see" it, being given to someone as a special gift. These are all examples of "seeing" things on a day-to-day basis, without intentionally tapping into the gift. Then, of course, you will be able to intentionally tap into your clairvoyance through meditation and other similar strategies.

Daydream

Daydreaming is one of the best ways to let your imagination run wild. When you find yourself daydreaming, give yourself permission to let it run free for a while. See where your daydreams take you. Practice letting your visuals get really strong and clear and see where it takes you. Daydreams are our clairvoyant skills at work on their own, and though they may not necessarily be telling you any particular message, they can be entertaining and interesting to partake in. Additionally, they help you get used to tuning into your imagination and letting it take control, rather than always trying to be in control. When you let yourself freely daydream without concern about what you "should" be thinking about or what you "want" to be thinking about, then your third eye gets to take charge.

When you are actually having a clairvoyant experience, you are going to be required to let your third eye take over and control the information being given to you. If you try and tamper with it or take control back, you might inhibit the quality of the message, therefore, alter what was being "told" to you through the visual. It is important that you practice relinquishing this control and letting your imagination take over sometimes.

Create Through Imagination

We won't go excessively into detail on this one again, but the art of expressing your creativity is a great way to tap into your clairvoyant abilities. If you really want to exercise clairvoyance and strengthen your skills, then you need to practice letting your mind completely take over. Think up something in your head and let it flow naturally through your hands. Do not try and control it or take over or perfect it in any way. Instead, just let it all flow out on its own. This allows you to learn to let your imagination take over as well, which as you just learned, is extremely important if you are going to be able to channel messages through clairvoyance.

Meditation Methods

Meditating is a great way to tap into your clairvoyant abilities. You can meditate with the intention of "daydreaming" from your meditative state, or you can even meditate and practice doing guided visualization meditations. Guided visualizations typically comprise of an audio track where someone speaks to you as they guide you through a specific vision. This could be anything from going into a field and sitting among the flowers to going to a specific place and meeting with your spirit guide. There are many different types of meditations you can embark on with guided visualization, and each one can help you exercise your clairvoyant muscle. Since you are guided through specific visualizations, you are able to exercise your mind's eye and practice seeing different details within' your imagination. This allows you to strengthen this muscle which will increase your ability to actually "see" through your third eye. This way, when you are having a clairvoyant experience, you will be able to see a little more detail and see more clearly than you might if you don't practice "seeing" with your imagination.

Practicing with Physical Objects

Another great way to practice tapping into your clairvoyance is by picking up old objects or going to old places. When you do this, take the time to sit and clear your mind for a few minutes. Then, focus on the object or place and see what comes to mind. If you notice anything in particular, such as a person, image, or particular vision, try and explore that image. See what you can notice about what you are seeing in your mind. For some people, they may be able to visualize a particular picture or moment, for others they may be able to visualize a lot more. It can take some time before you are able to fully visualize everything you are experiencing, but it will certainly be helpful in allowing you to learn how you can control the visions, summon them, and see them more clearly. It also helps teach you to have faith in your visualization and trust what you are seeing. When you are new it may be uncomfortable and so you try and convince yourself what you are seeing is not real or that you are unclear on what it is so you may have "made it up". The more you practice, the more natural it will feel and the more you will feel confident in what you are seeing and trust that you have not made it up but that they are organic visions of a time in the past.

Listen to Your Other "Clairs"

Honing your other "clairs" will help you practice with your clairvoyance as well. For example, if you are stronger with clairsentience than clairvoyance, consider what clairsentience experiences come up for you and how they might relate to any sparks of clairvoyance you may be experiencing at a particular time. See if they coincide or make sense together, and how they contribute to the greater "image" of what you are experiencing. If you can comprehend them and make sense of them then there is a good chance that what you are seeing is accurate and you can begin to trust it a lot more.

Developing your clairvoyance can be a lot of fun. Since the third eye is related to "seeing", many people want to develop their metaphysical seeing abilities. Everyone with a third eye has this ability, just like everyone has the ability to develop any of their clair-abilities. It can take some time and some focus, but when you have accomplished the task then you might find that being clairvoyant can be extremely entertaining and even enjoyable. For many, it even becomes their career as they become mediums and use their clairvoyance as an opportunity to communicate with people's loved ones on the "other side". Regardless of why you want to develop your clairvoyance, it can be highly rewarding and you should take your time and certainly invest in this process. It can be well worth it.

Clairvoyance Meditation to Open the Third Eye (10 minutes)

Clairvoyance meditation is a crucial part of opening your third eye and keeping it open as frequently as possible. This is a simple technique that can be surprisingly effective when done on a regular basis. The main thing to focus on with this exercise is going to be visualization. Those who are naturally visual people, meaning that if they hear the word apple they naturally picture an apple in their mind's eye, will likely find this exercise easy as it will strengthen a skill that they already have. It is especially important for those who don't naturally have this trait to practice this type of meditation on the regular as this deficit may make it more difficult for you to open your third eye than it otherwise might be.

If you have thus far struggled with the meditative exercises provided then you may find that this exercise will make it easier to see out of your mind's eye than it has been previously. Those who are not great visualizers will naturally need to exude more patience and determination in order to see the results they are looking for.

The first thing you will need to do is ensure you are in a quiet comfortable spot, you don't necessarily need to be standing, laying down is perfectly acceptable, just be sure you don't fall asleep in the process. Once you are properly settled, the next thing you will need to do is close your eyes while taking several deep, relaxing breaths; in through your nose and out through your mouth. A common mistake made by those who are new to meditation is to take breaths that are far too shallow. In order to correct this mistake, you can place you hand on your stomach while you breathe, stopping only when you feel your stomach stop expanding. Doing so will help you to get into the habit of breathing properly.

Once you are breathing properly, the next thing you are going to want to do is to close your eyes and visualize the number one. This one can be any size, shape or color that you wish just as long as you do everything you can in order to ensure it really sticks in your mind.

While performing this meditative exercise it is likely that you are going to begin to feel a tingling sensation in your forehead, somewhere between your eyebrows. This is the feeling of your third eye opening and is a natural part of the process. Once you start to have this feeling you will know that you are on your way. With enough practice, your third eye will remain open and you will have a variation of that feeling all of the time.

Once you have this feeling you are going to want to keep your mind clear of everything except the number one and hang onto it for as long as possible. If your mind starts to wander, don't force it and instead work on building up your mental fortitude over time.

If you don't feel anything, that's alright too. You likely just need to improve your ability to visualize, which means that if you keep up with this meditative exercise on a regular basis then you will eventually find the success you seek.

CHAPTER 8:
Mistakes To Avoid

Since the process of awakening your third eye is so personal, there are very few mistakes that you can make when you are doing it. However, there are a few that are common and can actually be considered mistakes. If you are wanting to awaken your third eye, you should be aware of these mistakes so that you can avoid them in your own journey.

Rushing the Process

Many people become so excited about what life with an awakened third eye can be like that they want to rush the process and get to the end. Unfortunately, this actually destroys their ability to truly awaken their third eye. Instead, they may feel frustration or disappointment or confuse other things for their third eye. This forced experience can really destroy the entire purpose of the process and can make it very unenjoyable for the person experiencing it.

The purpose of awakening your third eye is to have your own journey towards connecting with your inner self and the universe. Although this is an incredible outcome, the process is every bit as important as the result. If you want to awaken your third eye, you need to be willing to take your time and do it properly. This is not something to be rushed for the "status" of the results. Instead, you should understand that this has nothing to do with status at all.

Someone who is truly awakened understands status is a mere illusion, and rushing the process will not earn you status, but rather will destroy your results.

Comparing Your Experience to Someone Else's

This journey is so personal that there truly is no way to compare your experiences to someone else's. While sharing is enjoyable and even beneficial, wondering why your experiences have not been the same can be exhausting and can take away from the experience as a whole. You need to be willing to divorce the idea that you should be having the same experience as others or that you are wrong if you don't. Your experience is uniquely yours, just as theirs is uniquely theirs.

Discrediting Your Experiences

Many people discredit experiences they have relating to their third eye because they are afraid to admit that they are actually having the experiences. Just because you want them and are working towards having them doesn't mean the entire process isn't sometimes a little surreal or illogical. When you are awakening your third eye, try not to brush things off as "coincidence". Part of awakening is realizing that coincidences aren't real and that everything happens for a very valid and logical reason, even if you can't see the logic in what has happened. You will eventually understand, but in the meantime, don't try and find reasoning for everything by labeling them with words such as "coincidence". Instead, hold space for the true reason and allow yourself to go forward without having to know why certain things happened. Don't discredit your experiences.

Focusing Too Much on the Third Eye

As we have discussed previously in this chapter, you need to ensure that you are always giving yourself enough time to focus on the grounding part of the process as well. Excessive focus on your third eye without grounding and connecting to the physical plane can result in overstimulation which can lead, increased and unwanted visions, anxiety, being overwhelmed, seeing an excessive number of things that aren't there, and even feeling a total disconnect from the physical realm. You might feel as though when you are walking your head is "in the clouds" and this can lead to a great deal of anxiety. If you begin to feel like this, you can reverse the symptoms by focusing on grounding and bringing yourself back down to Earth. Give yourself a break from third eye meditations and focus specifically on rooting yourself back into your physical reality.

Being Ashamed of Your Journey

Some people who begin to embark on the journey of spirituality and awakening the third eye experience a sense of shame around their journey. This is typically a result of going against what was taught to them as a kid. Sometimes they believe that seeing things that aren't actually there would be interpreted as them being crazy, so they are ashamed to admit to their journey and share it with other people. If you are experiencing feelings of shame, you should seek towards healing these feelings. This would be a good place to start when you are healing your third eye during the awakening process. You should also seek to connect with other people who have awakened their third eye so that you have people who can help support you during the journey. This can help you feel more confident and supported as you go through this, as it can sometimes feel vulnerable which can lead to the shameful feelings that some people experience.

Ultimately, the best way to avoid making any mistakes during the journey is to truly tune in and keep it personal. Let yourself follow your intuition and your heart and trust in what they are telling you. If you feel guided to seek support from others who have gone through the journey themselves, or who are actively going through the journey, then you should listen to this guidance. As long as you honor yourself and your journey, you should feel completely supported and fine. If anything feels like it is not going right or you are feeling out of alignment, take the time to tune into your intuition and see what you need to do in order to adjust your course and find a more comfortable space for yourself.

Conclusion

Awakening your third eye is part of growing down your spiritual path and can have many incredible benefits. It allows you to increase your spiritual intuition, hone your mediumship and psychic abilities, and learn to lead a more spiritually whole life in alignment with your higher self and the universe. Individuals who are tuning into their spiritual self often look to connect with their third eye as this serves as the mind-body connection and can help them feel more authentic and whole.

Awakening your third eye is a process that takes time and should not be rushed. When you are awakening your third eye, you should honor that it is a unique journey, much like our journeys through life are. It is not beneficial to compare your journey to someone else's or to feel wrong for following your intuition. You are the only one who is fit to guide you through your journey in life, and you should honor that. You are the only one responsible for you.

Despite being the one entirely responsible for your own journey, it may sometimes be difficult to know where to go or what to do. Resources such as this book are wonderful materials for helping guide you along your path. It is important that when you are reading these resources you take the time to navigate them using your intuition. Pick the parts that feel right for you, and use them as a guide instead of a rulebook. Allow these to be the resources that help inspire you to venture further into your authentic self and explore who you truly are. This will ensure that you get the maximum benefits from your resources.

It is important to understand that just because this journey is unique does not mean it needs to be isolated. Many people wish to involve others in their journey by either seeking out mentors, reading books, or making friends who are on similar paths. This is a natural part of the journey and should be honored, not avoided. There is no shame in sharing your journey and allowing others to become involved in it. This is a natural part of life and a natural part of being a human. You are entitled to desire support and community in your life, and there is no reason why you should ever feel the need to deny yourself of this.

Finally, remember that the journey through awakening your third eye is one that should never be rushed. There is no "end result". Even once your third eye is opened and you are successfully using it, there is always more to learn and more to explore. Life is an evolution, and so is the process of awakening your third eye and learning to maintain your connection with it. Never rush the process. Instead, take your time and enjoy each stage. Life is a beautiful journey and each day is a vital part of that journey.

www.ingramcontent.com/pod-product-compliance
Lightning Source LLC
Chambersburg PA
CBHW071409070526
44578CB00002B/527